A Note to Parents and Teachers

Eyewitness Readers is a compelling new reading programme for children. *Eyewitness* has become the most trusted name in illustrated books, and this new series combines the highly visual *Eyewitness* approach with engaging, easy-to-read stories. Each *Eyewitness Reader* is guaranteed to capture a child's interest while developing his or her reading skills, general knowledge and love of reading.

The books are written by leading children's authors and are designed in conjunction with literacy experts, including Cliff Moon M.Ed., Honorary Fellow of the University of Reading. Cliff Moon spent many years as a teacher and teacher educator specializing in reading. He has written more than 140 books for children and teachers, and he reviews regularly for teachers' journals.

The four levels of *Eyewitness Readers* are aimed at different reading abilities, enabling you to choose the books that are exactly right for each child.

Level 1 – Beginning to read
Level 2 – Beginning to read alone
Level 3 – Reading alone
Level 4 – Proficient readers

The "normal" age at which a child begins to read can be anywhere from three to eight years old, so these levels are only general guidelines. No matter which level you select, you can be sure that you're helping children learn to read, then read to learn!

A DK PUBLISHING BOOK
www.dk.com

Project Editor Penny Smith
Art Editor Susan Calver

Senior Editor Linda Esposito
Senior Art Editor Diane Thistlethwaite
Production Melanie Dowland
Picture Researcher Andrea Sadler
Jacket Designer Margherita Gianni
Illustrator Chris Forsey
Indexer Lynn Bresler

Reading Consultant
Cliff Moon, M.Ed.

Published in Great Britain by
Dorling Kindersley Limited
9 Henrietta Street
London WC2E 8PS

2 4 6 8 10 9 7 5 3 1

Eyewitness Readers™ is a trademark of
Dorling Kindersley Limited, London.

A CIP catalogue record for this book is
available from the British Library.

ISBN 0-7513-6264-6

Colour reproduction by Colourscan, Singapore
Printed and bound in Belgium by Proost

The publisher would like to thank the following for their
kind permission to reproduce their photographs:
Key: t=top; a=above; b=below; l=left; r=right; c=centre

Ace Photo Agency: Front jacket; **Brown Brothers**: 22b, 33b, 36–37;
Corbis UK Ltd: Front jacket, 4cla, 6tl, 8cl, 11br, 11t, 20tl, 20bl, 21b,
25br, 27b, 31tr, 31cr, 32tl, 34b, 39t, 42tl, 46bl; **The Granger
Collection, New York**: 26tl; **Hulton Getty**: 2br, 9cra, 10tl, 10bl, 12bl,
14tl, 15br, 19tr, 19br, 21cr, 25t, 34tl, 41br; **Mary S Lovell**: 6clb, 19t,
38b, 40b, 46br, 47crb; **Popperfoto**: Reuters 43tr, 45tr; **Telegraph
Colour Library**: 18tl, 46tl; Ian McKinnell 36tl; J. Reardon 18cl;
Masterfile 21tr, 44bl; **Topham Picturepoint**: 30.

Grateful acknowledgment to Mary S Lovell for the loan of photographs
used in her book *The Sound of Wings: The Biography of Amelia Earhart*

Contents

DK EYEWITNESS READERS
PROFICIENT 4 READERS

FLYING ACE

THE STORY OF AMELIA EARHART

Written by Angela Bull

DK

London • New York • Sydney • Delhi

Roller coaster girl

Amelia Earhart gazed up at the roller coaster. Its steep, looping curves seemed almost to touch the sky. Amelia tensed with excitement.

"I want to ride on it!" she cried. Her mother looked doubtful. Amelia was only seven.

"I'm not going to," said Amelia's four-year old sister, Muriel. "You'll have to try it without me."

Then Amelia's father came to the rescue.

"I'll take you, Amelia," he said. "We shouldn't miss it. Here we are at the St Louis World's Fair and this roller coaster ride looks more fun than anything else."

Father and daughter got into the car and then jolted to a start. Slowly they climbed the first curve.

Then they plunged down faster and faster. Amelia screamed with delight. How silly of Mother and Muriel to stay on the ground, she thought. They could be whirling through the air like her.

Her eyes shone as she climbed out after the ride.

"It's like flying!" she exclaimed. Little did she know, she had found the way in which one day she would become world-famous.

Keeping cool
The World's Fair was held in hot weather and lots of ice cream was sold. To make it easy to eat, the first edible cones were invented.

Train travel
Steam trains first appeared in the US in the 1820s. They had dining cars and sleeping cars for rich passengers.

Birthplace
Amelia's grandparents' house still stands above the fast-flowing Missouri River. It is now the Amelia Earhart Museum.

The Earharts returned to Kansas City, USA, where Amelia's father worked in a railway office.

"Let's make our own roller coaster," Amelia suggested.

With the help of Muriel and an uncle she built a wooden track which she nailed to the shed roof. Next she found a small cart and hauled it up onto the roof.

Amelia scrambled on board and zoomed down the track. The moment she landed she jumped out and hauled the cart back to the roof. The sense of flying was wonderful.

Amelia's whole life was a bit like a roller coaster, with its ups and downs. She was born in 1897 at her grandparents' lovely home in Atchison, Kansas.

She lived there for much of the time with her mother, sister and wealthy grandparents.

But she often went to live with her father in his poorer home near his job in Kansas City. Amelia's mother resented her husband's lack of money and his habit of drinking too much. She stayed away from him for months at a time.

No alcohol
Drinking problems caused misery to many families. In 1917 the US government voted in favour of prohibition – an alcohol ban.

First flight
The first hot-air balloon to carry people was launched in France in 1783.

First plane
In 1903 Orville and Wilbur Wright built a plane called *Flyer*. In it they made the first controlled powered flight. It lasted just 12 seconds.

Amelia was an adventurous, active girl who liked to ride, skate and shoot. She and Muriel attended a good school and learned to be polite and well-mannered.

Amelia was still a child when she saw her first aeroplane at the Iowa State Fair. Planes were still new inventions then. They were tiny, unsafe constructions covered in canvas. They could not go very far or very high. Amelia was not impressed. "Just rusty wire and wood," she would later say.

Amelia's grandfather died. Then later, when Amelia was fourteen, her grandmother died too.

The old lady had been afraid
Amelia's father would drink
away any inheritance.
So her will stated that
no money would go
to Amelia's mother
while Amelia's
father was alive.

Kestrel
in flight

Man flies
glider, 1896.

Without money, Amelia's
mother was forced to return to
the husband she did not always like.
Instead of comfort and happiness,
Amelia and Muriel
had to settle for
a bare house and
a poor school.

Copying birds
People tried to
copy birds but
could not make
flapping wings
work. So they
used fixed
wings instead.

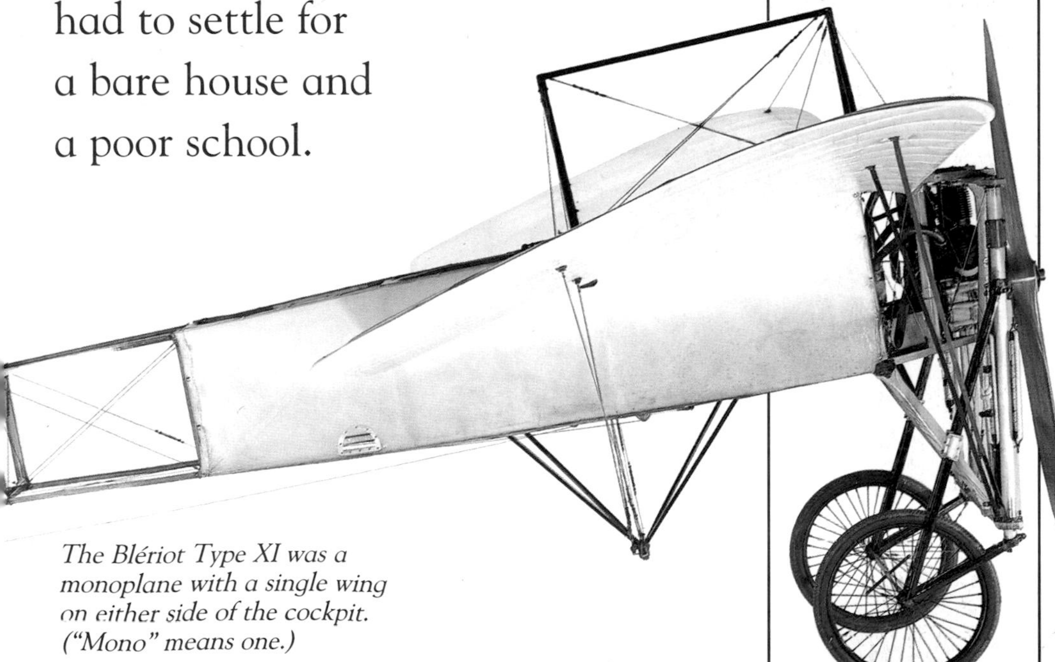

The Blériot Type XI was a
monoplane with a single wing
on either side of the cockpit.
("Mono" means one.)

Woman's work
Mary Pickford was a star of silent films. She played so many love scenes she was known as "America's sweetheart".

Nickname
US soldiers were called "doughboys" because their uniform buttons looked like dough cakes.

As her life changed, Amelia changed too. There was no fun at home for a penniless family. Her father was often too drunk to take her to parties and other places. She missed her old friends and became a loner.

She knew she would have to fight her own way out of the misery. Maybe the best way was to study for a good job. Amelia worked hard at school, and read and wrote poetry.

Most girls at that time did not worry about careers. They planned to marry and have children. Amelia wanted more than that. She searched through newspapers for stories of women with good careers. She knew women could achieve as much as men. She wondered what her own career would be.

Amelia went to college as World War One raged in Europe. She read about the gruesome horrors of war.

Soldiers wore masks to protect them from poison gas.

Taking care
Nurses looked after wounded, dying soldiers in the flimsy huts of field hospitals. Soldiers were sent back to the fighting if they got better.

Thousands of soldiers were wounded and killed by shells, bullets and poison gas.

American and Canadian soldiers were among those suffering terrible injuries. Amelia was concerned and wanted to help. Her classmates were not surprised when Amelia decided that nursing wounded men was more important than studying.

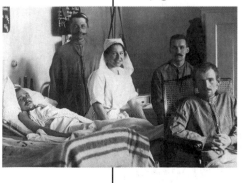

Air acrobatics
During World War I pilots used tricky moves to avoid enemy fire. The Immelmann Turn was a steep climbing manoeuvre.

Famous pilot
"The Red Baron" was a German pilot. He fixed a machine gun to the front of his plane and shot down 80 aircraft before being shot down himself.

Amelia moved to Toronto, Canada, and spent almost a year working in a military hospital as a nursing aide. She scrubbed floors and handed out medicine and food. She worked long hours and grew pale and thin.

It was a great treat when, one day, three military pilots took her to see the planes at a nearby airfield. The planes were small and fragile, but hundreds of them were used in the war. And the best pilots were now famous figures.

Amelia's nursing job ended soon after the war ended in November 1918. Military pilots also lost their jobs and many bought unwanted air force planes. They used them to earn money at air shows.

In those days flying was a new and exciting entertainment.

Ordinary people rarely saw a plane and few had the chance to fly. Air shows were popular – crowds gasped as pilots performed aerial rolls, wing walking and parachute jumps.

Amelia too was thrilled by the air displays. She could see that flying was dangerous, but it fascinated her.

Down to earth
Not all pilots survived air-show stunts. But they had more chances than World War I pilots. Every night there were empty places at air-base dinner tables. These belonged to war pilots who did not come back.

Early flights

For Christmas 1920 the Earharts gathered in Los Angeles, California. Amelia's father had stopped drinking and her parents were trying to make a new, happy life together.

Amelia and her father visited an air show at Long Beach. As Amelia watched the planes swoop and dive she felt a chill of excitement. She realized then what she wanted. She wanted to fly!

But this was 1920. Women were expected to look after husbands and homes and nothing more.

Taking control
US women, including Elizabeth Cady Stanton, fought for the right to vote in elections. They finally won the right in 1920.

Flying was rough and dangerous. Planes were primitive, unsafe and often crashed. Yet Amelia felt strangely drawn to flying. Her father agreed that she could take a short flight.

Amelia was flushed with excitement as the pilot took off. From high in the sky she could see the ocean and the Hollywood hills. The sight was so inspiring she was sure she wanted to be a pilot.

Famous sign
The original Hollywood sign said "Hollywoodland" and advertised a housing development.

Fashion
In the 1920s women's fashion discarded long dresses and waist-squeezing corsets. Young women became flappers and wore dresses that showed their legs.

Going forward
Engines are used to power propellers. These mini spinning wings thrust a plane forward.

But how could Amelia learn to fly? Try Neta Snook, she was told. Neta gave lessons.

Neta, one of the few woman pilots, watched Amelia walk towards her. Amelia wore a smart suit and white gloves. Neta eyed the unsuitable clothes doubtfully, but still she agreed to give Amelia a lesson the following day.

Dressed now in riding breeches, Amelia climbed into the dual-control plane.

Neta talked to Amelia about flying. Then she taught her to taxi across the ground and take off. Suddenly Amelia was in the air! She felt wonderful. Neta was impressed. Very few people learned how to fly a plane as quickly as Amelia had.

In fact Amelia's reckless confidence was alarming. She soared upward or dived beneath high-tension wires without showing any fear.

After a few days Amelia bought a leather coat to cover her smart clothes. It soon became creased and oil-stained as Amelia hung around the airfield finding out how aeroplanes worked. Everything to do with flying and planes was interesting to her. Amelia was happy now that she had found her purpose in life.

Wood work
Early propellers were made of wood. Some war-plane propellers were covered in brass to protect them from enemy fire.

Plane safety
Air lanes – or
invisible roads in
the sky – have
been used since
1922. Pilots are
given specific
times they can
fly these routes
to prevent mid-
air crashes.

Traffic control
Air-traffic
controllers
direct thousands
of planes that
take off and
land each day.
They make
sure a runway
is clear for
each plane.

Once Amelia could fly, she
wanted her own plane. She took
odd jobs, saved every penny, and
borrowed what she could. By her
middle twenties she had raised
enough money to buy a tiny plane.
It was called *Canary* because it was
painted bright yellow.

Neta, who was still flying with
Amelia, thought the plane was too
light to be safe. It was not a good
plane for a beginner.
However, Amelia was
determined to have it.

In her early flying days
Amelia had several small
accidents. They scared
other people, but Amelia was not
worried about them.

Once she crashed *Canary* as
she was taking off. Amelia bit her
tongue but was otherwise unhurt.
She crawled out of the damaged
plane, then powdered her nose.

Neta Snook and Amelia in California

Rudolph Valentino

News in 1921
Film stars such as Rudolph Valentino and Charlie Chaplin often made the headlines in 1921. A new snack – crisps – became famous too.

Charlie Chaplin

A plane crash – even a minor one – was a big news story in 1921. Amelia told Neta they must look nice in case a newspaper reporter arrived to interview them.

Later that year Amelia made her first solo flight. The takeoff was awkward, but she managed it. Then she flew up high over the airfield. Amelia was happy. Now she was free to be alone in the sky as much and as often as she liked.

First taste of fame

Record breaker
Lindbergh
crossed the
Atlantic in a
plane that was
built for him in
just two months.
It was called
*The Spirit of St
Louis* because
St Louis
businessmen
financed
the flight.

*Charles
Lindbergh*

In May 1927 Charles Lindbergh
became the first person to fly
solo across the Atlantic.
He stayed awake for more
than 33 hours to fly his plane.
Instantly he became a celebrity.
Other people tried to copy his feat,
but only four succeeded while
14 died in crashes.

Lindbergh's publicity was
masterminded by George Putnam.
Putnam was a publisher specializing
in real-life adventures.

After Lindbergh's flight, a
rich American named Amy
Guest contacted Putnam.
She wanted to sponsor the first
woman to fly the Atlantic.
She asked Putnam to find
"the right sort of girl". This
meant someone attractive and
confident enough to handle
the fame that would follow.

Friends told Putnam about Amelia and he invited her for an interview.

Amelia charmed him, so Putnam offered her the Atlantic flight. She would not fly the plane herself – a professional pilot would handle that. Amelia would be the captain. She would keep the log, writing in it what happened during the flight.

The plan must be kept secret in case another woman heard and made the crossing first.

Concorde
This modern-day plane travels faster than the speed of sound. It crosses the Atlantic in less than three hours.

Amelia and George Putnam planned the flight in detail.

Ocean liner
In the 1920s it took five days to cross the Atlantic by ship. Some ships were like luxury hotels, with swimming pools, saunas, cinemas and ballrooms.

Plane sailing
Seaplanes sit on floats and take off and land on water. They have rudders at the back so they can be steered on water.

Amelia agreed to make the journey. She heard the plane was called *Friendship*. It had pontoon floats instead of wheels in case it had to come down in the water.

Friendship was moored in Boston Harbour. Amelia and the other two crew members boarded it from a tugboat. The pilot, Bill Stultz, climbed into his seat at the front of the plane. He started the engines, then *Friendship* lumbered into the air.

Louis Gordon

Amelia Earhart

Bill Stultz

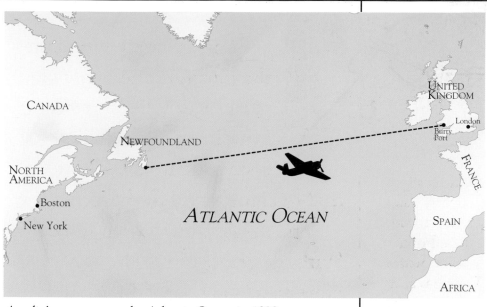

Amelia's route across the Atlantic Ocean in 1928

They flew to Newfoundland where the trans-Atlantic flight would begin. But in Newfoundland bad weather grounded them. For 13 days the crew was stuck. The wait was frustrating, tedious and stressful. Stultz coped by drinking too much.

Amelia took command. She made Stultz drink black coffee until he was sober. And she insisted on leaving the moment the weather was clear. So on June 17, 1928, they boarded the plane again. *Friendship* spluttered upwards. The crossing had begun!

Deadly waters
The Northern Atlantic is freezing cold. It was here that the *Titanic* hit an iceberg in 1912. The ship sank with a loss of 1,523 lives.

Up, up, and on and on they flew. Amelia was glad of her leather coat as they passed through chilling fog.

Suddenly they hit a snowstorm. Ice covered the wings. Stultz went into a dive, throwing Amelia across the cabin.

Day turned into night and night into day. The radio stopped working. Fuel was low. They should have sighted land by now.

Several ships cut across their path. They circled over one ship and Amelia dropped messages. The notes asked for their position. But the messages fell into the ocean and were lost.

All three peered through the windows, anxious and tense. Suddenly Bill's face lit up in a smile! He could see land ahead.

Dress sense
Early planes did not always have covered cockpits. Pilots wore warm leather coats, helmets and gloves. Goggles protected their eyes from biting winds. Some goggles were tinted to reduce glare.

The relief was enormous. Bill
made a perfect landing in the sea
near Burry Port in Wales. He went
ashore first and phoned the press.
By the time Amelia reached land, she
was famous. Two thousand
people rushed to see her.

On her way home
Amelia was welcomed in
London. In New York
George Putnam organized
a ticker-tape parade
for her, with torn paper
thrown at her open car.

Homecoming
A ticker-tape
parade was
a traditional
welcome for
a hero in
New York.

The Atlantic – solo

Black Thursday
In 1929 prices on the US stock market crashed. Some people lost everything.

1930 brides
Most women married in their early twenties, so at 33, Amelia seemed old.

Amelia was aware she had only been a passenger on *Friendship*. Any woman could have done it. She felt she needed an achievement of her own. After the flight she was well paid for public appearances. So in 1929, a year when many were short of money, Amelia bought a new plane, a Lockheed Vega.

In 1931 she married George Putnam. He had managed her publicity and advised her on her speeches and clothes. They spent time together and had grown close.

With her private life settled, Amelia began planning her great adventure. "Would you mind if I flew the Atlantic alone?" she asked Putnam one morning.

Putnam did not mind – in fact he was enthusiastic. A solo crossing by a woman would set a new record.

Amelia could write a book and earn a lot of money. Putnam decided that May 20, 1932, would be the ideal day. It was the fifth anniversary of Lindbergh's crossing.

Air race
In 1929 Amelia also organized a women's cross-country air race. It was dubbed "The Powder-Puff Derby".

Night flying
Pilots used the instrument panel for safe flying. The panel had an altimeter to show the plane's height and an artificial horizon to show if the plane was going up, down, or side to side.

As the day neared, Amelia flew to Newfoundland, her starting point. She knew she risked her life, but she wanted to prove that a woman could make the journey.

She took off safely, then as night fell, her altimeter failed. Without it Amelia could not tell if she was a safe distance above the ocean. She was in danger but she kept going.

She flew into a storm. Flames spurted from a cracked exhaust pipe. Amelia was cold and frightened but she did not turn back.

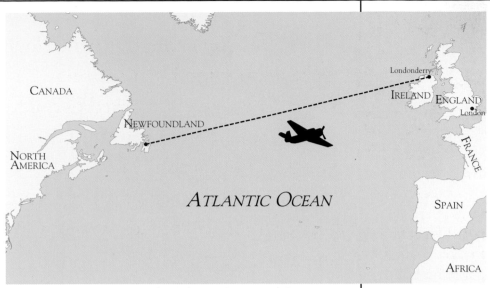

Amelia's solo route across the Atlantic Ocean in 1932

Amelia climbed to avoid clouds. Then ice formed on the wings. Suddenly the plane spun downwards! Down and down it fell, with Amelia desperately trying to regain control. After a 3,000-foot drop Amelia righted the plane. Just in time!

But then the fuel gauge jammed and fumes filled the cockpit. Dizzy and unsure of her fuel, she knew she had to land soon.

Then she saw a wonderful sight. There was land right beneath her! Amelia had made the crossing.

Downward spin
Air-show pilots perform spins by flying slowly. When air flows too slowly over the wings the plane "stalls" and falls towards earth.

THE ILLUSTRATED LONDON NEWS

The Copyright of all the Editorial Matter, both Engravings and Letterpress, is Strictly Reserved in Great Britain, the Colonies, Europe, and the United States of America.

SATURDAY, MAY 28, 1932.

THE FIRST WOMAN TO FLY THE ATLANTIC ALONE: MISS AMELIA EARHART AND HER 'PLANE AT CULMORE, NEAR LONDONDERRY, WHERE SHE WAS FORCED TO LAND.

Miss Amelia Earhart (Mrs. G. P. Putnam), the famous American airwoman, flying from Harbour Grace, Newfoundland, with Paris as her destination, had to land in a ten-acre field at Culmore, some two miles from Londonderry, Northern Ireland, on May 21. Thus she did not carry out her intention to make a lone flight across the Atlantic—in which connection it is interesting to note that her feat took place on the fifth anniversary of the solo Atlantic-crossing by Lindbergh. The third pilot who has made a solo crossing by air is Squadron-Leader Bert Hinkler. Miss Earhart has now flown the Atlantic twice—another record. On the first occasion, which was in June 1928, she was a passenger with Messrs. Wilmer Stultz and Louis Gordon. The airwoman spent the night in Ireland. On the following day, the Sunday, she was conveyed by air to Blackpool, and thence to Hanworth.

The next day
Amelia taxied her plane around the field for news cameras. She climbed out and the crowd threw hats in the air. Newsfilm of this was shown at cinemas. It was said to be Amelia's actual landing.

She landed in a field, where a man was herding cows. He told her she was near Londonderry in Ireland. He was astonished when she said she had come from America!

30

Amelia telephoned Putnam who alerted the press. As Amelia travelled home through Ireland and England, excited people mobbed her. In London her plane was displayed in Selfridges department store.

Back in the United States Putnam organized more lectures and public appearances for Amelia. She got involved in running new airlines and designing clothes for active living. She was a real celebrity, even staying at the White House with President Roosevelt and his wife.

Amelia was one of the best-known women in America. But by the age of 35 she was worried about how quickly she could react when flying. She was afraid she might be slowing down.

She wanted to make another big trip to prove to everyone that she was still as good as ever.

The President Franklin D Roosevelt's social reforms helped many US families.

Talking point Amelia was friendly with the president's wife, Eleanor, who spoke out for women's rights.

Amy Johnson
This pilot was the first woman to fly solo from England to Australia. When her plane's canvas wings tore, she fixed them with sticking plasters.

Crackups

After the Atlantic crossing, Amelia never received as much praise again. With the passing of time, flying was no longer such a novelty. Other women pilots broke records too. Amelia was not quite as special as she used to be.

Amelia's next long solo flight was from Hawaii to California. The takeoff from Hawaii was terrible. The Vega was weighed down with fuel. Its wheels sank in the mud before the plane jolted upwards.

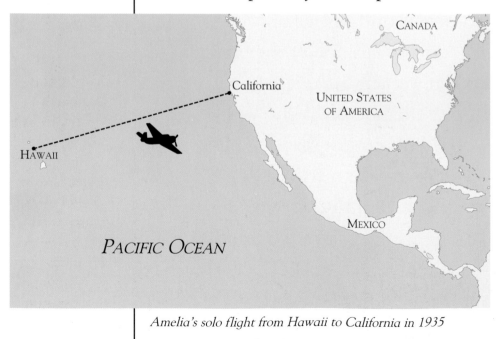

Amelia's solo flight from Hawaii to California in 1935

Amelia lost her way and had to ask a ship for her location. When she eventually landed in California she was thankful to climb out of the cockpit alive.

Critics said the flight had only been a publicity stunt to attract attention. They thought the poor takeoff and faulty navigation showed that she was not in full control of her plane. Her days as a heroine seemed over.

Amelia climbing into the cockpit of her Lockheed Vega

Navigation aid
A compass has a dial marked north, south, east and west. It also has a magnetic needle that always points northwards. Navigators use compasses to work out where they are.

Wind factor
In Amelia's day, wind made navigation difficult. It could blow a plane off course or make it travel faster or slower than the speed shown on the instrument-panel dials.

Although her flight from Hawaii had been criticized, Amelia never thought of giving up flying. Her achievements were not just for herself. Flying was her way of showing that women could do the same things that men did.

Putnam still organized lecture tours and media interviews for Amelia so people remembered her.

Amelia spoke to the press throughout her career.

Amelia wanted to be known, but she realized that she needed new achievements to keep up her position as a famous woman pilot.

Amelia had had five "crackups", as she called crashes, but not even these were enough to stop her flying. Luckily she had never been badly injured and her planes had always been repaired. Now, with the flight from Hawaii behind her, Amelia began to consider what she would try next.

She began to plan a flight that no one had attempted before. She wanted to be the first woman to fly around the world at its widest point. Her flight would roughly follow the equator, travelling from east to west.

Amelia's attempted flight around the world from east to west in March 1937

The equator
This is an imaginary line around the middle of the globe at its widest point. The equator is 40,076 km long. It is the hottest part of the Earth because it is closest to the Sun.

35

Setting course
The Sun rises in the east and sets in the west. Navigators used the Sun to work out directions by day. At night they used stars.

After its tough journey, Amelia's Vega had dangerously cracked wings. She was lucky to still be alive! With her savings, Amelia bought herself a new plane. It was a big, powerful Lockheed Electra.

The Electra had extra fuel tanks, better radio equipment and a hatch through which a navigator could steer by the sun and stars.

Unfortunately Amelia never mastered the radio equipment.

Nor did she know enough of the beeps of Morse code to transmit messages. The day would soon come when she would regret these failings.

Amelia got the Electra on her thirty-ninth birthday and spent five weeks in practice flights. She found the plane and its equipment difficult to handle.

News of Amelia's planned flight leaked out, but Amelia denied it. "All applesauce!" she declared airily. She could not risk a rival pilot making the flight before her.

SOS

●●● ─── ●●●

Coded message
Morse code uses dots and dashes that can be tapped out. Different combinations stand for different numbers and letters. Three dots, three dashes, then three more dots represents SOS, a call for help.

NR 16020

Amelia's Lockheed Electra 10E had its registration code on the tail.

Coral islands
Many small islands in the Pacific are made by marine creatures called corals. New corals grow on old, forming solid island structures.

So Amelia prepared for her first attempt to fly around the world in secret. She would travel from California to Hawaii, and then on to tiny Howland Island. From there she would continue her westward journey all the way back to America.

Amelia decided to take three crew members on the first stage of the journey. She needed expert help to find Howland Island so she chose navigator Fred Noonan.

Paul Mantz, Amelia Earhart, Harry Manning, and Fred Noonan before the around-the-world attempt

Irish saint's day
Amelia took off for Hawaii on 17 March 1937, St Patrick's Day. Noonan wore some shamrock to celebrate his Irish ancestry.

When Amelia was ready, Putnam alerted the press. They watched a successful takeoff from Oakland Airfield in California. After 15 hours and 51 minutes Amelia and her crew landed safely in Hawaii.

After refueling Amelia was ready to take off again. But the plane swayed down the runway then tilted over. A wing smashed and a wheel broke off. The Electra stopped and Amelia emerged, white-faced.

Noonan calmly folded his maps. He would be ready to go again whenever Amelia wanted, he stated.

But the Electra was too badly damaged to fly. This around-the-world flight was over.

Strong wheels
Early planes used car wheels for takeoff and landing. Then, as planes became heavier, pressed-steel wheels were used. Wheels were also positioned further apart so the planes would not topple over.

Saying goodbye
Amelia left
Putnam a letter.
In it she wrote,
"Women must
try to do things
as men have
tried. When
they fail, their
failure must be
but a challenge
to others."

Into the blue

The failed attempt only made Amelia more determined to fly around the world. Huge oceans and hot tangled jungles would not stop her. Refueling on primitive runways would not put her off.

Putnam agreed that she should try again. However, this time she would fly west to east. This would leave the difficult Pacific crossing until she felt completely in control of her plane. Noonan agreed to go too.

On May 21, 1937, the Electra was ready.

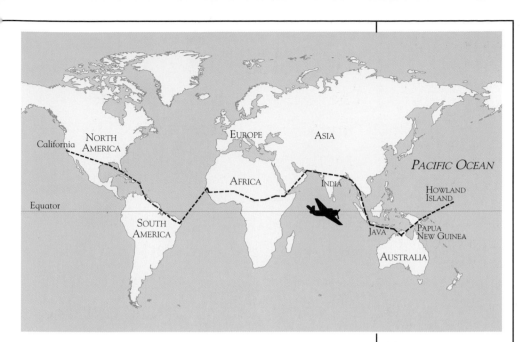

Amelia's flight around the world from west to east in June 1937

Amelia flew eastwards from California to Miami, Florida.

In Miami, Amelia discarded some Morse equipment because neither she nor Noonan could operate it. She also left behind the extra radio equipment that she had not needed on her previous trips.

Amelia was afraid this second around-the-world flight might fail. She dreaded growing old and told a reporter, "I won't feel completely cheated if I fail to come back."

Radio message
A microphone turns the sound of a voice into an electric signal. This is sent to the receiver. When the caller says "over" the other person can speak.

On 1 June, 1937, Amelia took off from Miami airport. She and Noonan flew to South America, then across to Africa.

Tight fit
Amelia's cockpit measured less than 1.5 m in any direction.

Bedbugs
These feed on human and animal blood. Young bedbugs are almost see-through. But they turn dark red after they have had a good meal of blood.

The plane was cramped and noisy. Noonan sat at a map table behind the cockpit. When he wanted to communicate with Amelia he passed her messages on the end of a fishing line. It was easier than trying to shout.

They crossed Africa, where storms and head winds made it difficult to hold the plane on course. When they landed they slept in primitive airfields. Amelia and Noonan were hot, uncomfortable and bitten raw by bedbugs.

Even though Noonan was with her, Amelia felt alone. Fuel fumes in the cockpit made her sick and she grew very tired.

They pressed on over India, where they battled with monsoon rains. When they reached Java after three weeks and twenty thousand miles, Amelia was exhausted. She was thankful to stop while the plane was overhauled. There were still another 15,000 km to go.

Monsoon rains
Monsoon winds bring torrential rains to India. These often cause floods. The monsoon starts in May and dies down in October.

Putnam planned for Amelia to land back in the United States on the Fourth of July. He even arranged for her to broadcast from San Francisco on 5 July. Amelia knew this was impossible.

She flew from Java to Lae, in Papua New Guinea. This was the takeoff point for the final part of her journey across the Pacific.

She left Lae on 2 July. Watchers saw the Electra for the last time as it lumbered into the clouds. It was heavily laden with fuel. Its destination was tiny Howland Island.

Amelia and Noonan had only a basic idea of how to use the radio.

Fourth of July
This day is Independence Day in the US. It celebrates the end of British rule in America.

Yet for the Pacific crossing Amelia had to communicate with the coastguard cutter *Itasca.* This ship would give her locations and weather reports.

The *Itasca* tried to guide her, but Amelia seemed unable to hear its transmissions. At last Amelia's voice crackled through the static. She was not sure where she was, she told them, and fuel was low.

Through the early hours of 3 July the *Itasca* picked up messages of increasing desperation. Then there was silence. No one ever heard from Amelia or Noonan again.

Sea patrol
Coastguards work on ships and wear uniforms, like sailors in the navy. But coastguards have their own jobs to do, including searching ships for smuggled goods, weapons and drugs.

Pacific islands
There are many uninhabited islands in the Pacific. Palms grow beside beautiful empty beaches. But behind the beaches vines twist into dense jungle. The waters around the islands are full of sharks.

What had happened to Amelia? The most probable answer was that the Electra ran out of fuel and crashed into the Pacific. A huge search-and-rescue operation was launched involving nine naval ships and more than 60 planes.

Newspaper headlines tol of Amelia's disappearanc

AMELIA EARHART DOWN AT S
'ARSHIP CATCHES FAINT SIGNA

Rallies Men Bond Broker
Back to W

Flyers Lost In Mid Paci
Gasoline Supply Runs O

ribune LATE CITY EDITION

3 Earhart Search Planes
Launched Off Colorado;
Weak Signals Buoy Hope

Aviatrix, Aid Gone Since E
Morning; Coast Guard Sear
Searches Lonely Ocean

Troops Clash

U. S. Battleship Reache
Phoenix Islands Where
2 Flyers Are Believe
Marooned on Re

Lexington Speeds
To Widen Search

DAILY MIRROR, TUESDAY, JULY 6, 1937

Liberty Scout Wins 2d Delaware **Sports 6 Star**
THE EVENING SUN

Budge Wins 3 Titles, Wimbledon Record
**RADIO MEN HEAR EARHART'S
VOICE FAINTLY ASKING FOR AID.**

**Amelia Floating,
Radio Sputter**

WASHINGTON, July 5 (AP).—A message to C
Guard headquarters today said intercepti
radio signals "indicated possibility Earhart

Baltimore American

EARHART RESCUE PLANES DRIVEN BAC
BY STORM; 6 AIR SQUADRONS JOIN H

Missing Pacific Flier And Navigator

One ship searched for wreckage along what was thought to be the Electra's flight path. Faint radio signals were reported, apparently coming from islands 560 km southeast of Howland.

Aeroplanes surveyed the islands, but found nothing – or almost nothing. One plane spotted "traces of recent habitation" on Gardner Island, but no Amelia.

Amelia was so famous that the mystery could not be forgotten. A theory surfaced that she was spying on Japan for the US government and she had been shot down, imprisoned or killed. But no evidence for this was ever produced.

Perhaps Amelia did crash onto Gardner Island. We may never know. She was a brave, record-breaking pilot who showed what women were capable of. And her disappearance remains a mystery.

Radio messages
Hoaxers tried to join the action. They sent made-up messages from Amelia.

Flight recorder
Today's black box, which is in fact orange, records what the crew says.

Stamp out
Amelia continued to be famous. In 1964 a stamp was issued in her memory.

Glossary

Aerial rolls
When aircraft rotate sideways without losing height or direction.

Black box
A flight recorder used by people investigating a plane crash.

Cockpit
This houses the flight instruments used by a pilot.

Compass
An instrument with a magnetic needle that is used to find directions.

Crew
The people in charge of a plane, including the pilot and navigator.

Cutter
A small, fast boat used by the coastguard.

Dive
A steep, nose-down descent by a plane during which speed builds up rapidly.

Dual-control plane
A plane with two sets of controls. A learner uses one set. The instructor can take charge by using the other.

Equator
An imaginary line around the globe at an equal distance from the north and south poles.

Flight path
The course of an aircraft through the air.

Head winds
Winds that blow directly against the course of an aircraft.

Hot-air balloon
A balloon that rises when the air inside it is heated. It flies because hot air is lighter than cold air.

Log
The detailed record of an aircraft's journey.

Microphone
A device that picks up sound and transmits it in electrical waves.

Morse code
A code system in which letters and numbers are represented by dots and dashes and transmitted by sound signals.

Navigation
The process of working out the route an aircraft should take.

Parachute
A giant canopy that slows a person falling to earth.

Pontoon floats
Watertight, box-like attachments under a seaplane that enable it to float.

Propeller
A twisted wood or metal plane part. It spins at the front of a plane and thrusts the plane forward.

Publicity stunt
A method of gaining public attention for a person or thing.

Publisher
A person who turns an author's written work into a printed book.

Rudder
The flat steering equipment at the back of a plane or boat.

Social reforms
Measures taken to improve people's lives including better schools and pensions.

Spin
A spiral nose dive.

Ticker tape
Paper ribbons used to record stock prices.

Transmission
A message sent through radio waves.

Tugboat
A small powerful boat used to tow craft at sea.

Women's rights
The idea of giving women the same rights and pay as men.